Rookie
reader

ALL KINDS OF KIDS

Written by Christina Mia Gardeski
Illustrated by Bob McMahon

CP
Children's Press®
A Division of Scholastic Inc.
New York • Toronto • London • Auckland • Sydney
Mexico City • New Delhi • Hong Kong
Danbury, Connecticut

FOR MY PARENTS, WHO HAVE FIVE KINDS OF KIDS,
AND FOR PAUL, THE BIGGEST KID OF ALL!
WITH LOVE—C.M.G.

TO LALANE
—B. Mc.

Reading Consultants
Linda Cornwell
Literacy Specialist

Katharine A. Kane
Education Consultant
(Retired, San Diego County Office of Education
and San Diego State University)

Library of Congress Cataloging-in-Publication Data

Gardeski, Christina Mia.
   All kinds of kids / written by Christina Mia Gardeski ; illustrated by Bob
McMahon.
      p. cm.—(Rookie reader)
   Summary: Children may be different in how they look, what they like to do,
and even what they like to eat, but they all have great smiles.
      ISBN 0-516-22370-4 (lib. bdg.) 0-516-27381-7 (pbk.)
      [1. Individuality—Fiction. 2. Stories in rhyme.] I. McMahon, Bob, 1956- . ill.
II. Title. III. Series.
PZ8.3.G174 AI 2002
   [E]—dc21   2001003561

There are all kinds of kids.

Some kids are girls.
Some kids are boys.

Some kids are quiet.
Some make lots of noise.

7

Some kids are tall.
Some kids are short.

Some kids play music.
Some play a sport.

Some kids have brown hair.
Some kids have red.

Some kids ride bikes.
Some ride chairs instead.

Some kids share.
Some kids tease.

Some kids like pizza.
Some like peas.

And one thing is true
if you travel for miles.

All kinds of kids
have all kinds of smiles!

23

WORD LIST (43 WORDS)

a	have	noise	smiles
all	if	of	some
and	instead	one	sport
are	is	peas	tall
bikes	kids	pizza	tease
boys	kinds	play	there
brown	like	quiet	thing
chairs	lots	red	travel
for	make	ride	true
girls	miles	share	you
hair	music	short	

ABOUT THE AUTHOR

Christina Mia Gardeski was a quiet, tall, red-headed kid who liked to ride bikes and eat pizza. When she grew up she became a lifeguard, water safety instructor, and teacher, which gave her the chance to work with all kinds of cool kids. They, along with her nieces and nephews, were her inspiration for this book. Christina is currently a writer and editor of children's books. She lives in northern New Jersey, sharing smiles with her husband, Paul, who makes lots of noise playing the drums.

ABOUT THE ILLUSTRATOR

Bob McMahon lives in sunny southern California with his lovely wife, Lalane, who lets him draw funny pictures whenever he wants.